Bird Watching for Beginners

Everything You Need To Know To Get

Table of Co[ntents]

Chapter 1

What Is Bird Watching

Chapter 2

The History of Bird Watching

Chapter 3

How To Bird Watch

Chapter 4

Equipment For Bird Watching

Chapter 5

Prominent Contributors to Bird Watching

Chapter 6

Bird Watching Organizations and Societies

Chapter 7

Bird Watching Etiquette

Chapter 8

Science and Bird Watching

Chapter 9

Bird Watching Influences
on the Environment

Chapter 10

Backyard Birding

Chapter 11

Birding Census Techniques

Chapter 12

Bird Watching Books And Publications

Chapter 13

A Personal Tale: Bird Watching 101

Chapter 1

What Is Bird Watching

What exactly is bird watching? If you go walking through the forest and spy a bird, are you bird watching? Do you have to be knowledgeable in the study of birds before you are considered a bird watcher? Bird watching or birding is basically defined as the observation and study of birds with the naked eye or through a visual enhancement device like binoculars. Though some may disagree, bird watching and birding is essentially the same thing, both are the observation of birds in the wild.

In the birding community though, there is some disagreement about grouping the two terms into the same category. Many deem bird watching to be different than birding on quite a few levels. They feel that mere bird watchers deem it more as a past time and don't pursue it with the same enthusiasm as a birder. It is felt that bird watchers are more content to observe more locally and don't invest in the same grade of equipment as that of a birder. In short, birders don't tend to rank themselves in the same category as bird watchers.

Birders feel this way because they tend to invest in higher technology equipment and are dedicated to study birds for more than general observation. Many birders will purchase optical equipment such as spotting scopes. They may even invest in auditory equipment in order to identify the species by year. They take note in moult, distribution, migration patterns, and habitat. Birders are also more prone to travel in order to pursue their passion of birds. It's basically the same sport; one group just takes it a notch higher than others.

So what do you do when you go birding? Birding is a little more involved than merely looking at birds, though you do observe them.

Birding also included learning to recognize the birds and identify them. As with any subject you study, you begin to understand the birds and gain knowledge of what they're doing while in nature. Many people outside the birding world don't seem to realize that there are over 800 different types of birds.

Obviously everyone has to start somewhere when they begin a new hobby or sport. You aren't going to automatically know everything there is about birds without researching them. For many it takes years before they gain a firm understanding of all the aspects of birding, and all are still learning as new information emerges. Just for clarification purposes, going to the zoo and looking at birds is not birding. Birding is the observation of birds in the wild or natural habitat, not in cages or captivity.

So do you have to be some retired person with loads of money in order to go birding? Not at all, anyone who has an interest can watch birds. It's something that you can start out young and continue through adulthood. It's an activity that can involve the whole family. There is no encompassing age or demographic when it comes to birding. It's actually proving to be one of the fastest growing activities in America and is also extremely popular in Britain as well.

So why should I observe birds? Why do other people sit and watch birds? Birds are a beautiful species that are absolutely amazing, especially while in flight. It's breathtaking to just sit and watch them soar so high above the earth, so effortlessly in the clouds. In ancient times, the bird was considered a foreseer of the future. Now in or world of technology, they can still let us know what we can expect in the environment. They can often help us build a stronger bond with nature.

Are there any the benefits that come with birding? To the beginner and novice in birding, there are a variety of benefits that you can benefit from. First and foremost is the fun and pleasure that can be found in birding. There is also a certain satisfaction that comes from searching for the different species of bird. It's almost like hunting without harming your prey. Birding can also be a fun family activity that helps to strengthen the bond between children, parents, and grandparents. Also it helps introduce children to nature and aid them in gaining a respect for it as well.

Birding is a versatile sport that can be either done with or without others. If you are seeking companionship, then birding can be a great social activity. You can share your interest with friends, family, or even join a birding club. If you seek the chance to get away from everyone for some well deserved solitude, then that is also an option. It's perfectly acceptable to go birding alone. You can go explore nature with the only sounds coming from the birds you are observing.

So now that you have an interest in birding, where do you go? For beginners it can be as simple as stepping out your front door. Start with your own neighborhood; observe the birds in your own backyard, so to speak. Watch their behaviors, look at what they're doing. Once you've done that, try to start identifying the birds you see. Start paying attention when you travel, especially if there is a change in environment. It's likely that you'll see new species of birds when you travel quite a ways from home. This is just the start of your birding experience.

Chapter 2

The History of Bird Watching

The question of when bird watching or birding was officially considered a past time, hobby, or sport is hard to answer. No one really knows the true date that birding was defined, but many believe it to be around 1968. This isn't just a lucky guess; it's believed to have become an actual past time in 1968 due to the first known birding publication was produced in that year. This publication was called The Bird Watcher's Digest and could be describes as more of a newsletter than anything. There were only about 5 pages of literature, but it was the first official document of a bird watching nature. This new literature was founded by the "American Bird Watchers Association" or the ABA as they deemed themselves. With this newly proclaimed association quickly came America's official interest in bird watching.

Once the American Bird Watchers Association was established so was a membership status. You could buy a years' membership for the nominal fee of $3.00. So what did this newly found literature encompass for the sport of bird watching? For the first time in publication, there was a publication not only providing documentation about birds, but also listing the rules for this new found sport. In 1969 the title changed from The Bird Watcher's Digest to simply Birding as became the popular term for bird watching, and is still in print today. The magazine prints and distributes their issues every other month to their readers.

As more issues were published the official guidelines for birding were defined. Also in 1969 it was proposed that the ABA that originally stood for the American Bird Watchers Association be changed to the American Birding Association. By the end of that year there were already 128 members participating in the ABA as well as newly appointed officers in the organization. Between the ABA and the Birding publication, birding was becoming a popular sport. With the rising popularity would also bring a change in both the publication as well as the organization.

In the short period of three years the publication was ready to take on a more professional appearance to the bird watching world. Birding was made into a more journal like publication in 1971 and no longer took on the appearance of the mere newsletter form that it originated from. The new publication gave readers a variety of articles to read. There was a total expansion on pieces that delved into the true art of birding, no more were there just species lists and opinion pieces, but true reporting pieces that brought a new form of excitement.

The July/August edition of Birding in 1973 brought quite a buzz to the birding community. It was the first issue to have pictures printed in the publication. It was also the first issue to report on the first convention held by the ABA in Kenmare, North Dakota. The edition printed in July/August help define many of the new aspects of the ABA such as their checklist report, newly elected leaders of the ABA, and the newly ratified laws of the ABA. This new issue was popular for many reasons and was a wealth of information to the birding community that was quickly growing in number. The ABA's membership had grown from their original 128 members in 1969 to 1,872 in 1974, a difference of 1744 in as little as five years.

The 1970's brought some evident changes to both Birding and the ABA. In 1976 for the first time since the first 5 page publication in 1968, Birding printed a publication that was 400 pages; a vast different from its meager beginnings. Also, the ABA recognized their second president, Arnold Small. In 1977 the cover of Birding began to take on a different appearance, printing beautiful covers that awed many bird enthusiasts. There was also a bit of disturbance in the birding community between east coast versus west coast. It seems that many were annoyed with the Californian birding styles that were constantly being praised.

From its beginnings in 1968 to 1988 Birding had gotten behind schedule in its publications as well as harder to understand. It was up to Editor Paul Lehman to bring the journal back to its origins and back on track.

He focused on making the magazine easier to understand for readers and outlined a number of focal points to expand on. In 1989 Lehman made good on his commitment and came out with a very different looking magazine that boasted a completely new layout. Lehman helped take the magazine back to being the true form of communication for the birding community.

In 1992 the ABA focused on the demographics of their member. They soon realized that a majority of its members were over 40, as a whole, they were getting older. Alarmed with the statistics, they focused on gaining a younger demographic by offering reduced membership as well as youth camps. They realized that without some sort of change, the sport of birding could begin to dwindle. Although membership was up to 10,200 active members, the concern of gaining young birders was still an issue for the ABA community.

It being 2007, almost four decades have

passed since the first publication of The Bird Watcher's Digest¸ now known as Birding. The hopes of the ABA have been recognized, and the art of birding is rapidly growing among North America and Canada. As many have been taking notice, with growth also comes change. The new birders don't necessarily hold on to the same ideals as the older generations of birders. The new generation is also more focused on the newly emerging technology that many old timers might shrug away from. The Birding magazine is also feeling the impact of the new generation due to their updated staffing crew. Change is in the air both in the ABA community as well as Birding publications, but change is not always a bad thing, with change comes a new opportunity for all of those in the birding community

Chapter 3

How To Bird Watch

If you really have the desire to bird watch there is a certain way to go about it for beginners. Remember, as mentioned before, anyone can take up the sport of birding, it just takes time to get acquainted with the ins and outs. The first step is to acquire a pair of binoculars, adjust them to your preference, and try them out a few times before you actually need them. The binoculars are so that you can get a better view of the bird without having to get so close that you might scare it off. Also, not all binoculars are created equal; there are different types that offer different functions. It might even be helpful to ask a salesman to explain the differences between different models.

It's good to get in the habit of locating birds with your eye first, without the aid of the binoculars. This is important because you have a greater range of vision with the naked eye than you do with binoculars initially. When focusing primarily through binoculars you might miss the chance of locating the bird due to the smaller field of view.

Binoculars have the primary objective of narrowing in on an object for better definition. It's wise to wait on using the binoculars until you have already found your target.

Now that you have the primary equipment needed, it's time to go look for birds. How do you find the birds? It's a good idea to learn the habitats of birds so you know what to look for. It's important to note that each species of bird have their own habitat preference, birds are much like other animals that in each breed, or species is different. Once you know what to look for and where to look, the task of finding birds will become much easier. It's also helpful to listen as well; you may often hear the bird before you see it.

So you've found your first specimen, what exactly are you looking for beyond identifying that it's a bird? Although it may be difficult to decipher, color is definitely something to look for when birding. If you have the opportunity to observe color, you are very lucky because normally it's hard to view colors correctly, even for the most seasoned birder. The difficulty in observing the correct color of a species is due to many factors such as lighting as well as shadows which make it hard to be accurate.

Size is another factor to consider when birding. Size can help you rule out certain other species quite quickly. For example it is quite obvious that a small bird such as a Mountain Blue bird wouldn't be put in the same category as a large bird such as a Heron or Hawk. Size can also be deceiving though. You must take into consideration the conditions that you are observing the bird in. If the bird is flying overhead, the size of the bird may appear much larger or smaller than it actually is. If you find yourself in this situation, it is sometimes helpful to compare the size of the bird to something equal in distance that you are familiar with such as a tree.

Shape and profile is also something to look

for when birding. It's highly suggested to invest in some sort of bird guide. A bird guide is easy to take into the field with you and will help you to identify birds. Once you become familiar with the certain characteristics of birds through the guide, you will be able to rule out certain types on shape and profile alone. A bird guide is also helpful when you are out in the field and spot a bird you are not familiar with. The guide provides information as well as pictures to help guide you through and is helpful to beginners as well as those familiar in the sport of birding. Once you become more comfortable you can graduate to the National Geographic Field Guide to the Birds of North America 3rd edition.

Also not required, but very useful are a notebook, backpack, and a hat. The notebook is for you to record what you see when observing. The more you write, the more you tend to observe, then later you can review your notes. The backpack is so you don't have to lug everything around by hand. You can also keep things such as bug spray, water, and a snack as well as anything else you might want to take along. The hat is obviously for your head. When out birding you are being exposed to the elements and the hat will help shade your eyes from the sun without interfering with your use of binoculars.

It's also helpful to find a check list for your area. This will help you know what to expect when birding. Checklists can be found through many state and national parks, as well as online through your local department of wildlife website. Birding.com also has checklists for every state and province in the United States, Canada, and every country in the world. This can be found by clicking on the bird checklists link and choosing your desired location.

Another fun way to get involved in birding is to find a birding trip in your area. Depending on where you live, sometimes local bird trips are advertised in local newspaper or magazines. These trips are usually led by a local park ranger or a member of one of the many birding and wildlife societies. You can look online at birding organizations for information or contact your local rare bird alert phone number; this can be accessed by state at birding.com which is quite a handy reference. When you call the number they first go through a list of rare birds in your area, and then sometimes mention any trips at the end of the call. Usually these trips are free of charge, but it is wise to check if there is a fee beforehand.

Now that you have a better understanding of bird watching or birding, it's time to go enjoy your newly discovered interest.

Chapter 4
Equipment For Bird Watching

Almost every hobby or sport needs some sort of equipment in order to fully participate and show your potential, birding is no different. Compared to many other hobbies and sports, birding is relatively inexpensive. Just like anything else, depending on how enthusiastic you plan to get into birding will determine how much you plan to spend on equipment. For the beginner or less enthusiastic birder all that is needed is binoculars, a notebook, and a field guide. For the more active and devoted birders, other equipment might be needed.

Binoculars

Every birder needs a good pair of binoculars in order to observe their target without disturbance. When looking for a good pair of binoculars there are a few thing you should know before you buy them. Those little numbers on a pair of binoculars such as 7x50, 8x40, or 10x50 do actually hold some meaning to a buyer. The fist number which is the smaller number stands for the magnification. The second number which is the larger one stands for the diameter of the front lens in millimeters.

To break it down simply, the bigger the number on the binoculars, the greater the magnification. So if you choose the 10x50 you are going to gain greater magnification than with the binoculars that are 7x50. So, does bigger mean better? Not necessarily in the art of birding. With binoculars bigger means heavier, where the smaller ones are lighter and easier to carry around with you. The larger magnification binoculars are better suited to when you are stable, not when you are moving around.

So which ones should be used for birding? It's not suggested to use the smallest magnification due to the reduction in light and smaller field of view. The best suggestion is to look within the range of the 7x35 or 8x40 binoculars. It's very possible to get a decent pair of binoculars at a reasonable price. Just remember to try them out before purchasing and cheaper isn't always the best route to take with binoculars.

Those who get seriously into birding tend to invest more into their binoculars and choose models that use range roof prisms. Higher end models that use the range roof prisms tend to be more compact and more user friendly than those that use porro prisms. Another important factor to take into consideration is the binocular strap, not something you wouldn't necessarily think about when a beginner. It's very important to have a binocular strap that is comfortable because you are going to have that weight strapped around your neck for possibly hours. You want make sure to have a strap that is wide and comfortable, or look into one that distributes the weight evenly.

Field Guide

A field guide is quite a useful tool to any birder. A birding field guide is a book that has been specifically designed to help the reader to identify birds. Field guide are also designed so that you make take it into the field with you. It normally has a compact design that can easily fit into a backpack or pocket. A field guide if full of information on birds. It not only describes the different species of birds, it also includes picture to make it easier to identify them. It also suggests what to look for when birding.

When looking for a bird field guide, it is important to find a guide that is particular to your region. There are bird guides that focus on certain areas such as Alaska, Colorado, and Michigan. It's important to remember that a certain bird species found on the east coast might not share the same habitat as those found on the west coast and vice versa. If you live in Florida and plan to do your birding there, then you should find a bird guide that features the species found in Florida in order to fully benefit from your bird field guide.

Checklists

A birding checklist is a bird list for areas all over the world. Checklists can be found through many state and national parks, as well as online through your local department of wildlife website. A checklist help to identify which birds are ingenious to a certain area. Birding.com also has checklists for every state and province in the United States, Canada, and every country in the world. This can be found by clicking on the bird checklists link and choosing your desired location

Spotting Scope

A spotting scope is a portable telescope often used in birding when not on the go. The magnification of a spotting scope is greater than that of binoculars and run in the range from 10x to 250x depending on need of the birder. This type of scope is generally used when observing birds on land, requiring a range of magnification not found in binoculars. A spotting scope is designed for wider fields of view and is great for long distance viewing.

Tripod

A tripod is a three legged stand for a spotting scope, used to stabilize and elevate the spotting scope. The tripod is used as a stand for the scope so that you can be hands free while birding. It also helps to keep it stable so you don't have to worry about losing your target.

Clothing

Clothing when birding can be essential. You need to wear the right clothing for the area and weather conditions when you are birding.

Foot Gear

Shoes are very important. When birding its imperative that you have the proper shoes on. Very often you will be walking extensively and need to be wearing shoes that allow for this with maximum comfort. Also consider that you might do some hiking in certain areas and need to be equipped with the proper foot gear for these excursions.

Chapter 5

Prominent Contributors to Bird Watching

Though the sport of birding is more a collaborative effort of many, there are a few people that stand out. These individuals have made various notable contributions to both the sport of birding as well as birding publications. These four have helped to increase the understanding and further the interest to many enthusiasts. It has to be noted though that many have contributed to the world of birding, and that these mentioned individuals are just a few in a long list.

Roger Tory Peterson

Roger Tory Peterson was truly an inspiration to bird enthusiasts everywhere. Peterson was born in Jamestown, New York in 1908. He went onto further his education at the Art Students League and National Academy of Design. He then went on to teach school in Massachusetts. In 1904 when Peterson was only 26 years old, he wrote the first modern field guide titled "Field Guide to the Bird" which resulted in inspiring many enthusiasts. It actually sold out its first printing in the first week alone.

Peterson went on to either write or edit close to 50 books on the topic of nature in one form or another. Peterson revolutionized the modern bird guides with a sense of clarity and understanding that failed to exist before him. Peterson was awarded every kind of American award existing for his studies and literature in natural science, ornithology, and conservation. Not to mention all the other awards and diplomas presented to him from both within the United States and beyond. Many have described him as one of monumental significance in the promotion of all living creatures and nature. Peterson died in 1996 while in his home in Connecticut.

Kenn Kaufman

Kenn Kaufman was born in 1954 in South Bend, Indiana. Kaufman had a love of birds from the early age of six. When he was sixteen he so loved the field of birding and was inspired by greats in the field such as Roger Tory Peterson that he withdrew from high school and began to travel North America in search of birds. In 1973 he set the precedent recording as many as 671 bird species in North America in as little as one year. He was the first to complete such a feat. He journey across North America encompassed around eighty thousand miles. A detail of his journey is recorded in

"Kingbird Highway."

Kaufman's main focus was on that of creating and expanding birding field guides. A few pieces of his work include "Kaufman Focus Guides: Birds of North America"," Lives of American Birds", and "The Peterson Guide to Advanced Birding". In 1992 he was recognized by the

American Birding Association when he was awarded the Ludlow Griscom Award for Outstanding Contributions to American Ornithology.

Phoebe Snetsinger

Phoebe Snetsinger was born in 1931 in Lake Zurich, Illinois. Snetsinger was an inspiration to many in the birding community. She is the first person to have seen over 8,000 species before she died. Her fascination of birding began in 1965 after observing a Blackburnian Warbler. Although interested, she did not begin to ardently pursue her birding fascination until 1981 when she was diagnosed with terminal melanoma. Presented with the dire news, she chose continue living her life while fulfilling her passion for birding.

Snetsinger threw herself into her quest to observe as many birds as possible before her time was up. She traveled all over the world while encountering all types of danger throughout her quest. It was during a birding trip in 1999 that Snetsinger was killed in a tragic car accident. During her travels she made it a habit to take notes of all her experiences as well as findings. After her death the book "Birding on Borrowed Time" was published in 2003 with accounts of Snetsinger's travels as well as her fight with an incurable illness.

Theodore A. Parker III

Theodore A Parker III was born in 1953 and raised in Lancaster, Pennsylvania. Parker became interested in bird watching while quite young, and at age 18 broke the record for observing more species of birds in one year that anyone else. He went on to attend college at the University of Arizona where he continued his birding expeditions. Parker had quite of skill when it came to identification, and quickly was deemed one of the best ornithologists around.

It's said that Parker had his own method when it came to birding that allowed him to expand his knowledge in both details and behavior. He was very generous with his knowledge and findings and regularly shared them with the birding community. Parker was killed in a plane crash in 1993 while in Ecuador. He was truly a marvel to the birding community that contributed greatly to the growth and knowledge of birding and identification.

Without the skill, knowledge, and contributions of these individuals, the birding community might not be where it is today.

It's through the works of these people, as well as every other contributor in the birding community that has allowed the knowledge to grow in such massive proportions to where it is today.

Chapter 6

Bird Watching

Organizations and Societies

One of the best ways for you to begin birding is to find other enthusiasts that can help you along as you start out. Birders are almost always willing to help you out and share their knowledge and tricks of the trade. If you don't personally know anyone who is into birding there are many resources available to help you find local birders. You can first see if there is a local Audubon society nearby, this can be done by visiting their web site at audubon.org or calling. It's very likely that there a local chapter in your area. If you don't find one through the Audubon Society you can also try local bird clubs or nature centers or visit birding.com to see if there are any organizations in your area.

The National Audubon Society

The National Audubon Society is a non-profit organization whose mission is to "conserve and restore natural ecosystems, focusing on birds, other wildlife, and their habitats for the benefit of humanity and the earth's biological diversity." The Audubon Society is over 100 years old with its origins dating to the 1900's being one of the oldest organizations of the kind. The Audubon Society has not only helped preserve many habitats, but has also been a guiding influence in legislation throughout the years.

Many acts have been brought to the attention of legislation as well as passed due to the influence of the Audubon Society. In 1918 the Migratory Bird Treaty act was passed by President Wilson which put in place the protection of migratory birds. In 1964 President Lyndon Johnson passed the Wilderness Act that set aside 9 million acres of protected wilderness. This was a major factor to protect wildlife habitats from the increasing population that threatened such areas. In 1973 the Endangered Species Act was passed by President Nixon. The Endangered Species Act allowed for the conservation of species on the brink of extinction. All these acts passed were a telling of the efforts put forth by the Audubon Society. Without their continuous determination throughout the last 100 years, many of the species we enjoy today would have tragically disappeared from the earth.

Preservation of animal habitats is not an easy task to accomplish, especially with the ever growing population and destruction of many natural habitats around the world. The Audubon Society recognized the need to rally their efforts into the protection of all animal species. In 1947 the Everglades National Park was established encompassing thousands of miles in the central Florida area. Protecting the Everglades has been a continuous battle for the Audubon. In 1974 the Lillian Annette Rowe Bird Sanctuary was opened in south central Nebraska becoming a home to many migratory birds such as the beautiful Whooping Crane. This sanctuary is actually owned and operated by the National Audubon Society. These are just a few of the victories of the Audubon in establishing habitats for our wildlife to continue on and prosper in; they continue in their fight for wildlife daily.

The American Birding Association

The American Biding Association (ABA) was formally known as the American Bird Watchers Association until 1969 when the name was changed to what it is today. The American Birding Association was a key element in the sport of birding and presenting it to the public. Before the ABA was formed in 1968 there were no formal publications on birding. Enthusiasts had to rely heavily on references from friends. It was extremely difficult to gain any information that would help in the process of identifying species as well as locating them.

Publications put out by the Audubon were mainly focused on conservation and little to do with bird identification. This all changed when the ABA was formed with the publication of the "Bird Watchers Digest" which was quickly changed to "Birding". It was through this publication that the guidelines for the ABA were discussed and agreed upon by avid birders. It was agreed upon that the main focus of the ABA would be the hobby and sport of birding. After about twenty years of this focus, it was finally agreed that the ABA would allow the topic of conservation to be addressed in addition to its primary focus of birding.

In the early years of the ABA, the "Birding" publication was the whole of the organization. Now with the passing of years, the ABA has grown to encompass a wide range of communications in the birding community. With a ABA membership you are entitled to publications, participation in conferences, conventions, travel related benefits, ABA tours, ability to purchase gear through ABA sales, and a change to get involved in the community; definitely a far cry from the early days of the ABA. The ABA is a great organization aimed at birding interests such as identification, listing, education, and conservation.

Association of Field Ornithologists

The Association of Field Ornithologist (AFO) was founded in 1922. The AFO is one of the leading societies of both professional and beginner ornithologists. They are committed to the scientific study as well as the circulation of their studies about birds in their natural habitats. The AFO is a membership organization devoted to bird conservation and study. The AFO is a great source of communication between the beginner and professional ornithologist.

For those not familiar with the term ornithologist, it is basically someone who studies all aspects of birds. They focus on how they live, feed, evolve, the biology of a bird, and how they are affected by the changes in environment. The AFO is one of the six major societies in North America. Upon becoming a member you are provided with the quarterly "Journal of Field Ornithology", AFO association newsletter, invite the AFO annual meeting, discounts, and a bimonthly newsletter. A very informative tool when one has an interest in the inner workings of birds.

Chapter 7

Bird Watching Etiquette

What etiquette or ethics code needs to be followed in birding? As with any other sport or hobby there is a proper etiquette when it comes to birding for the beginner and novice alike. Each society has their publications on etiquette while birding. So what exactly does this mean for you? It means that it's important to familiarize yourself with the proper etiquette with any sport or hobby you are looking to pursue, preferably before you do it. Ignorance isn't a good excuse when there is plenty of literature to inform people, even those just starting out their birding experience.

The Rights of the Bird

As far as the birds themselves are concerned, they have rights too, just as people do. It's important for you to aid in the safety and wellbeing of birds and their environment. You wouldn't want someone coming into your house and trashing it, the same goes for birds while observing them. All animals are astute and can sense a human's presence. Try not to agitate them while birding and don't put them at risk. This means that it might not be wise to take too many pictures if photographing and that it's not always the right time to use recordings.

It has to be reiterated that endangered species are a major concern throughout the world. That being stated, it's important not to use any other methods than observation with any species that is endangered, of special concern, or is considered rare. It's extremely important not to do anything to disturb such species that are already experiencing such issues. Also, keep your enthusiasm at bay while birding and do not disturb nests. Birding is the act of observing birds in their natural habitat, not touching or taking.

So you're out birding and had the good fortune to find a rare bird species. Although you are probably ready to shout it from the highest tree and inform every organization and society you can think of, there are other factors to consider before doing so. First take into consideration how the bird will be affected as well as their habitat. If you advertise the bird's location will the bird be at risk? Also, where exactly is the bird located? If you are on your Uncle Earl's farm, consider that he might not want tons of people trespassing on their land to see a bird. It's definitely exciting be the one to experience a rare find, but remember that one of the main focuses of birding is the welfare of the birds.

Laws and Rights of Others

When birding, it's important to consider the laws of where you are as well as respecting the rights of other people. It is not ok to trespass on somebody's property. This is a clear violation of someone else's rights, and can be a danger to you. If you happen to spot a bird that you wish to observe on someone's property, stop and ask if you can go on their property. Chances are that the owner will give you the ok if they have an understanding of what you are doing and wish to accomplish.

Become familiar with any pertinent laws in the area you are planning to go birding in. Every state and area has different laws; it's wise to educate yourself beforehand. There might be certain areas that the public cannot go, even to observe birds. It might be the case that the area you plan to explore is a protected habitat. There might be certain areas that don't allow vehicles. It's worth the time of doing a little research to avoid any penalties that might occur if you break any laws, rules, or regulations. Officials won't be impressed or swayed with the phrase "I didn't know".

Creating your own Habitat

Many birding enthusiast create a bird friendly environment in their own backyard so they may experience the pleasure of birding without going far. There are many things to consider when doing this. When you place a bird feeder or other structure it is very important to keep it clean. This is also true for any water of food you place in the structure. If you don't pay attention you might just be offering rotten food or water that should not be consumed.

If you plan on setting up a structure to bring birds to your area, you need to make sure that it safe before doing so. If you own a dog or cat and keep it in the same area that you plan to set up the structure or habitat, you may need to rethink your strategy. You don't want to create a habitat in a potentially dangerous area. The same consideration needs to be followed if there are any hazardous materials in the proposed area. It's important to keep the welfare of the bird in mind at all times.

When Birding in Groups

There is a difference when birding in solitude and when birding with a group. There are new things that the group needs to pay attention to. Everyone has to adhere to the basic etiquette in birding mentioned above.

When going as a group you now have to consider those around you and not interfere with their birding experience. It's ok to share your information with others, it's actually preferred, especially to those that are just starting out.

Unfortunately there might be instances where you see a fellow birder doing something that they should not. If the behavior is something that you know should not be done it might be upon your shoulders to get involved if it's necessary. If it comes to this, do so in a friendly manner if possible. Let the individual doing wrong know exactly why their actions are unsuitable and ask for them to stop it. If the individual chooses to ignore your warning, then take note of it and any additional information needed so you can inform the proper individuals.

It's important to be a good example, not only to your fellow birders, but also to those outside the birding community. It's likely that other birders, especially beginners will take notice or your example and strive to follow. It's important to follow what you teach, don't say one thing, and then do another. Be responsible and make sure the group size is reasonable. You don't want a horde of people tramping through a bird's habitat. It's also important to remember that other people outside your birding group may be out enjoying nature or some other sport, be respectful of others.

Even if you are the leader of the group, it's important to make sure that everyone is aware of what they are supposed to be doing as well as not doing. Anyone in the group should share any useful information about the area in which you are birding, especially if there are any no, no's. If you plan to go on a birding tour take heed that your tour guide knows what they are doing. It's their responsibility to make sure that birds come first. In all, have fun and enjoy your birding experience no matter where it is or who you go with. Just make sure to use the proper etiquette when doing so, this is so that everyone benefits, humans and birds alike.

Chapter 8

Science and Bird Watching

In a world where science is expected to explain everything and be everywhere, how exactly does it pertain to birding? Does birding have any impact on science? Does learning about the different species of birds help those in the world of science at all? All of these are good questions. It's important to learn how birding affects science and the world around us.

Ornithology is the science of birds. An Ornithologist is someone who studies all aspects of birds. They focus on how they live, feed, evolve, the biology of a bird, and how they are affected by the changes in environment. The field of Ornithology has been adapted due to the realization that birds are not only important to study for the love of birding, but they are also important in the world of science. Birds play a vital role in the world that scientists are continually defining.

Scientists have a whole system of studying birds. First they classify each bird in a seven step process. They use the classification system developed by Carolus Linnaus in 1758. This system breaks down each type of bird. For example, if you were break down the American Robin with this system, this is how it would look:

Level

Name

Description

Kingdom

Animilia

Animal

Phylum

Chordata

Animals with backbones

Class

Aves

Animals called birds

Order

Passeriformes

Birds that perch

Family

Turdidae

All Thrushes

Genus

Turdus

Similar Thrushes

Species

Turdus migratorius

American Robin

Now just think that they do this for every bird. Scientists and ornithologists put a lot of work and effort into their research. They are constantly classifying and re-classifying birds. Due to this science it's quite normal for birds to actually have two names. One is the bird's scientific name, which is usually in Latin. The second is the bird's common name which is usually how the bird is more commonly known. It's good to be familiar with this system because many checklists may use a combination of this information.

So now that you know what ornithology is and that scientists spend a lot of time studying and classifying birds, how exactly does birding help science? Through birding, information is acquired from beginners, novices, and ornithologists alike. This information helps determine changes in migratory patterns and decrease in certain species among many other factors. The combined information helps scientists determine how our environment is changing. When birds have to adapt to new conditions it then flags scientists to the conditions that caused the change. In turn, scientists can come up with solutions to these constant changes in our world which helps both animals and humans.

Chapter 9

Bird Watching Influences on the Environment

Due to the growing interest in birding throughout the last documented 100 years there has been an increase in caring for the environment. Bird enthusiasts began observing birds in their natural habitats. In the process they were also able to observe the effects that development and growth had on the environment. It was through this distress that organizations such as that of the National Audubon Society were formed. It became their goal to fight for the habitats of birds and other animals in effort to preserve our environment.

Because of conservation efforts and birding enthusiasts laws were passed to protect species that would have otherwise gone extinct. The Migratory Bird Treaty Act was a major win in 1918 to keep bird wild American birds safe. The endangered species act was passed in 1973 in hopes of keeping wildlife such as the bald eagle from dying out of existence. Multiple land acts have been passed in order to set aside land for wildlife. These organizations have aided in the fight to clean up the air in order to fight global warming. They brought to attention the need to preserve or natural elements such as water.

Birding organizations have fought endlessly to preserve many natural habitats around the world. The Everglades National Park is a well known habitat that was almost completely destroyed by population growth and development. Through the efforts of many organizations it was able to be saved, in turn sparing all birds and other animals that find their home there that would have simply died out. Conservation efforts have saved habitats such as this all over, in turn saving thousands of species, not only animal, but plant, insect, fish, and many others.

Without the help of many birding organization as well as other animal organizations, the world would not be what it is today. Our environment would be vastly different. Many animals, plants, fish, and insects would most likely not exist. They would only be something to read about in books, or something that older generations merely remembered. Birding has had a very positive impact on the environment. Those in the birding community continuously contribute their information and knowledge to each other. Organizations found in birding as well as other nature groups strive to improve our environments for the sake of the animal factor as well as the human factor, we are all connected.

Chapter 10

Backyard Birding

Many birding enthusiasts love to watch birds where ever they are. For this reason, many turn their backyards into a bird haven. This is fairly easy for anyone to do and provides the pleasure of looking out your back window and spotting an array of birds without having to leave your house. There are several steps you can take to make your backyard a bird paradise. There are both short term and long term steps to be taken to accomplish this. There are also several factors to consider.

Food and Shelter

First you need to make sure that your backyard is a suitable place for birds to dwell. If you house your dogs or cats in your backyard then it might not be a bird friendly environment. You really don't want to come out one morning with the hopes of birding only to discover Rover covered with feathers. Also it's not fair to your existing pets to have birds zipping in and out of your backyard while expecting your pets not to take a swat at them; it's in their nature to do so and really not fair to penalize them for it. You need to make sure that it will be a safe environment for the birds before trying to attract them.

You can then start with a bird feeder or bird house. It's important to note that depending on the bird's preferences, different bird houses will attract different birds. Some birds may not adapt to bird houses. You can do some research to see what type of bird house to get. The location of the bird feeder or bird house is also critical, chose a place that is safe. Once you get a feeder or bird house up it time to fill it with some food to attract the birds. Again, the type of food you put out will attract different types of birds. You may choose to offer a variety of food to attract many kinds of birds.

Water

Now that you have the food covered, there are many options for providing water to you feathered friends. Many feeders have a place to put water. Another option is to install a bird bath, bird fountain, or some sort of pond. Birds aren't too picky; anything that they can access that retains shallow water will make them happy. You can choose something inexpensive or choose to add to the value of your backyard and put in something that might be a little more costly, but adds to the appeal of your home. Just remember to change out the water regularly if you choose a method that offers standing water. It's also important to clean feeders and watering areas to avoid the spread of diseases between birds.

Plants and Trees

Now that you have the easy tasks complete, it's time to think more long term. Take a good look around your backyard. Are there trees, shrubs, and flowers? If your backyard is pretty bare there are plenty of things you can do to attract birds that will keep them coming back. You need to provide them with an appealing habitat, plus you can make your backyard look great in the process. Plant a variety of small trees and bushes. There are many types that certain types that offer food and nesting opportunities to birds depending on where you live.

For those in the Northeast a great bush to consider is the Highbush Blueberry which is a shrub. This bush can draw up to as many as 30 different species of birds such as the Brown Thrasher and Gray Catbird. It's a pretty shrub that will eventually offer berries to the birds when it matures. It also provides them with great nesting opportunities. The Eastern Red Cedar is a great tree if you have a large backyard. This tree can grow up to 65 feet and is a great home for many birds like the Ruffed Grouse and Yellow-bellied Sapsucker. The Eastern Red Cedar provides nuts and can attract many species.

For those in the Southeast the Arrowwood Viburnum is a shrub that produces berries in the late summer months. It's an attractive plant that also offers great nesting sites to various birds such as the Eastern Bluebird and American Robin. The Southern Magnolia is a beautiful tree that can grow as tall as 90 feet. It's a fruit producing tree that matures in the fall. The Southern Magnolia attracts different species such as that of the Red-bellied Woodpecker and the Northern Mockingbird.

For those in the Central Plains and Praries the Big Bluestem is a beautiful grass like plant that produces seeds as well as nesting opportunities for over 24 species of birds such as the Sedge Wren and Meadowlark. It's a plant that provides great cover and attracts many different song birds. The Gray Dogwood is a large shrub that can grow up to 9 feet. It provides fruit berries to birds such as the Northern Cardinal and Eastern Bluebird.

For those in Western Mountains and Deserts the Mesquite is a multi-stemmed shrub which can grow up to 15 feet and a single stemmed tree that can grow a tall as 40 feet. It provides seeds, cover, and nesting grounds to birds such as the Gambel's Quail and White-winged Dove. The Rocky Mountain Juniper can be considered either a shrub or a tree and can grow to 30 feet. It provides nutlets that offer birds such as the Northern Mockingbird and Evening Grosbeak great coverage.

For those in the Pacific Coast the California Wax Myrtle is a shrub or small tree that can reach 35 feet. It's a great source of food that produces fruit all year long, even during winter months. A bird to can benefit from this plant is the Yellow-rumped Warbler and California Towhee, amongst others. The California Wild Oak is a beautiful shrub-like tree that can reach 85 feet. You definitely need to make sure you have the room for this tree. It offers nuts and fruit to birds such as the Western Scrub Jay and Chestnut-backed Chickadee. It creates great coverage for the birds and is a very easy tree to maintain.

Depending on your area, another option for trees are fruit trees. This way both you and the birds can benefit. Great trees to consider are lemon, apple, and cherry. They offer birds the sweet blossoms followed by fruit. The birds can get their food from the tree and you can have a freshly grown apple when you like. It's a winning combination for all and a great way to grow your own fruit.

Flowers are another great idea that will not only attract birds, but will make your yard look great. This is especially a good idea if you are interested in attracting humming birds. Humming birds love the sweet nectar that flowers provide. It's good to plant a variety such as sunflowers, marigolds, and poppies. You can even look into adding vine-like plants that will add to the ambiance of your yard as well as attract birds. In the end, you garden will be breathtaking. You need to make sure to be adding native plants that will survive in your area and that birds will be comfortable with.

National Wildlife Federation

Once you have created your bird paradise you have the option of Contacting the National Wildlife Federation. They encourage home owners to create wildlife gardens for birds and other animals. They recognize the importance of giving back to wildlife what progress and development have taken away. When you are done creating your backyard you can check to see if it matches the guidelines of the National Wildlife Federation. If it does then you can get a National Wildlife Federation display that shows your contribution to the environment.

After all that work you now have a backyard that will attract birds for many years to come. You just might wake up to the sounds of birds chirping happily in the morning hours. You can sit and watch the birds while you eat your breakfast or drink your coffee. You can enjoy all the aspects of birding while sitting in your pajamas. Life is now great for the birding enthusiast

Chapter 11

Birding Census Techniques

There are different techniques you and may perform to census the birds in your area. A census or survey of the area can offer some great information. Many organizations perform these surveys in order to gain information to add to their knowledge of bird population biology, community ecology, and conservation efforts. These are techniques that anyone can perform, but preferably require a group to accomplish this task. You and your group can gather data on the size of a population of birds in your area. This can help you become more familiar with the different species in different regions if done in different cities or states, as well as different neighborhoods in your vicinity.

Variable Circular-plot Method

With this type of census you first need to designate the areas that are going to be surveyed. You can map out certain areas that might contain certain plant and tree life, for this example we will use 200 m distances. Next you need to decide on a time frame for the survey. Everyone participating needs to follow the same time established such as 15 or 20 minutes for each section. The timeframe might differ for larger or smaller areas. Remember that this is a slow and detailed process; take your time so you don't miss anything.

Once started, each bird that is observed needs to be counted and you need to estimate the distance from the bird in retrospect to your station. When counting, only count the birds in your station area, don't count any birds that might be flying around, unless it's apparent that they are in using the area to eat or nest. If you happen come upon birds and cause them to fly away, these birds do need to be counted. You also need to estimate their distance. Basically you are collecting a lot of raw data that will be reviewed when all station are completed.

To collect the data is may be useful to have a universal sheet to help with continuity between all the data collected. Below is an example of a data sheet that can be used and created on most computer spreadsheet programs such as Excel or be done by hand.

Station

Species

Distance

1

Yellow-rumped Warbler

8 m

2

Yellow-rumped Warbler

12 m

3

Yellow-rumped Warbler

25 m

4

Yellow-rumped Warbler

28 m

Once the data has been collected it is then time to analyze the data. First you need to plot the number of birds identified and the distance recorded from your data sheet like the one above. You need to make a list of the number of birds you observed in each 10 m circle

Here is an example of how to list them:

0-10m = 1

10-20m = 1

20-30m = 2

Next you need to figure out the density for each one. Below are calculations to aid in figuring this out. Due to varying of distance it is important to note that it's imperative to use concentric 10 m bands which are as follows:
0-10m = 314m2,

10-20m = 943m2,

20-30m = 1570m2,

30-40m = 2200m2,

40-50m = 2827m2,

50-60m = 3456m2,

60-75m = 6361m2.

This is important so that the data is consistent.

0-10m = 1 bird/314

m2 = 0.0032 birds/m2

10-20m = 1 bird/943

m2 = 0.0011 birds/m2

20-30m = 2 birds/1570

m2 = 0.0013 birds/m2

You then need to estimate the population density for each type of bird in the area you observed. You accomplish this figuring the densities inside the inflection point. The amount of people has to be added as well as summing the area. The plot graph below is an example of the results you will have at the end of the survey. Also you do a little research to get more complicated formulas for analyzing the data at various websites that explain this sort of census gathering.

Now that you are done plotting you now need to figure the habitat density. In order to do this you need to calculate the number of birds as well as the areas for each 10m band inside the inflection point. So for our example it would look like the following:

1/314 + 1/943 + 2/1570 = 4 birds/2827

m2 = 0.001415 birds/m2.

You are probably wondering what you now do with this information. You now need to convert it by birds/ m2 to birds km/ m2 . Don't be worried, this is quite simple, you take your last figure of 0.001415 and multiply it by 1,000,000 m2/km2 in which you get a total of 1415 birds/km2. Now the last step is only if more than one station was used. You then divide the density estimate by how many stations were used. So in this case it would look like the following 1415/3 stations = 472 birds/km2. Once you've made it this far you now have the results to your census.

This method is mainly used to get an idea of size and trend of forest bird populations. In many regions, this is the best census form to perform. One of the issues with performing a Variable Circular-plot Method is that it can be difficult to get a sample large enough to account for all the species in the area.

Variable-strip Transect Method

The Variable-strip Transect Method is another form of census that can be performed to evaluate birds in your area. In order to conduct this method you first need to a linear transect of a distance that needs to be determined before the census is performed. A transect is basically an imaginary line used that lets you measure the area you are conducting the census in. Once this is accomplished, the group participants walk this transect very slowly. Much like the Variable Circular-plot Method, observers need to record that they may see or hear as well as the distance from the transect line.

The same rules apply for birds in flight as the Variable Circular-plot Method.

You can use the same sheet to record data; just change the stations to transect lines. Again, after all the data is collected, you need to plot it much like you did for the Variable Circular-plot Method. The population density is different in this method. It is determined by calculating the densities for all strips inside the inflection point. You calculate the strip area by multiplying the strip width by transect length. An example would be 10m X 200 m= 2000m m2 = 0.002 km2. Each strip is 10 m in width since each strip extends 5m on both sides of the transect lines. Below is an example of a transected circle:

Getting your calculations for the Variable Strip Transect Method is very similar to the Variable Circular-plot Method. The main difference is that on your graph you will not be plotting density of birds vs. distance, instead you will plot the number of bird observed vs. distance. This is because all the transects have the same area. Also there is only one station you don't need to divide but the number of stations.

Chapter 12

Bird Watching Books And Publications

A great way for beginning birders, experienced birders, or anyone interested in birds to learn and gain knowledge is through reading. There are a ton of great magazines, books, and articles available on birds. They even offer such publications to different countries as well. Many of the organization and societies listed in Chapter 6 either publish magazines are recommend great birding literature. So what literature is out there for you to enjoy and expand your knowledge with?

Magazines

The American Birding Association or ABA has been closely linked to Birding magazine since its debut in 1968. When you become a member of the ABA you will receive bi-monthly issues of Birding. The magazine prints articles on a broad range of interests in the birding community. The ABA supported magazine features topics that run from field identification to bird conservation. This is a great magazine for any bird enthusiast.

They National Audubon Society also offers a magazine simply titled Audubon. This publication features many articles ranging from birds, wildlife, conservation, plants, and more. You can basically find information and reading on any topic relating to the environment and the species that inhabit the earth. Very interesting reading and the magazine website even offers articles not found in the printed magazine, labeled as web exclusives. This magazine is definitely a wealth of knowledge and information found in this publication.

Journals

North American Birds is another publication produced by the American Birding Association. This magazine has undergone a vast change of name in the past. It may also be knows as part of Bird Lore, Audubon Field Notes, as well as American Birds. This is a journal for birders. It provides readers with a summary of the ever changing view of North American's birding. This is a great resource for records, range, population dynamics, and many other items associated with the birding world.

Books

If you're looking for a good guide book then you might want to check out the ABA's website. They offer a ton of books at their online store. Even if you're looking for something else, you will probably find it there. They carry a variety of different birding books, guides, interesting stores, and travel related birding books. This is definitely a place to check when looking for a book on birds.

A book definitely worth getting is one I have mentioned earlier in chapter 5. The book is Birding on Borrowed Time by Phoebe Snetsinger. Snetsinger is mentioned during chapter 5 as becoming the first person to observe over 8,000 species. After her death the book Birding on Borrowed Time was published. The book is an account of her findings as well as her adventurous travels through the world while battling a terminal illness. This book is filled with valuable birding information as well as a touching story of a woman who lived her life for every second she was given.

Newsletters

Winging it is not a magazine, book, or journal. It is an informal newsletter aimed specifically at the American Birding Association members. This newsletter updates the members with any recent finding about birds and birding in North America. It also follows the news in other parts of the world and communicates it to the ABA members. This newsletter is a membership publication and has been providing the ABA members with interesting and pertinent news wince 1989.

If you're looking for a younger perspective then A Bird's-Eye View might be what you're seeking. A Bird's-Eye View is a bimonthly newsletter that is written by members of the American Birding Association who are students. This newsletter is nothing to scoff at. The young group of writers provides readers with topics on identification, field skills, optics, artwork, news, and many other areas of interest. Definitely a great source of information and enjoyable reading with a younger generations twist.

Internet

As mentioned many times throughout the chapters of this book, the internet is a great source for information. This is basically true for any topic since we live in a world where the internet is considered an information super highway. If you have access to the internet then it's a great way to gain information on birding. All you have to do is use a search engine, and with a click of the enter button your screen will fill with hundreds of websites, journals, and articles. Pretty much anything that has to do with birds, bird watching, or birding will instantly appear.

Even if you veer away from many of the main web pages such as the American Birding Association or the National Audubon Society, there is still a lot of information out there.

Fellow birders are eager to share their knowledge and findings with everyone. If you have questions, there are online forums where you can post it and have someone answer it for you. This is especially great if you are someone who doesn't have the time to call organizations or go to local meetings or clubs in your area. The internet can be extremely helpful and informative to a birder, whether they lack experience, or if their novice in the field.

It just has to be remembered that the internet is a place where anyone can post information. Because of this, some of the information posted may be incorrect or have flaws in it. Even those with the best of intentions can be wrong about certain things. If you are looking for thoroughly researched information, then it might be wise to stick to a well known organization.

Chapter 13

A Personal Tale: Bird Watching 101

There are so many people in the world that benefit from birding. Whether it is the sheer pleasure they experience when birding, or the love they have for nature; people who go birding all share a love for birds. Rebecca Snyder was no different in this aspect; she found a love for birding. What wasn't expected was how her love for birding would help her through her darkest hour. Rebecca shares her story and how discovering a love of birds helped turn her life around.

Finding my Way

After the divorce I just couldn't seem to find the enthusiasm for anything anymore. Being married for 27 years and then set aside for someone else was the most devastating trial in my life. After all when you're 49 years old, have had 3 pretty much grown children, you are not really expecting to be turned in for a younger model without much warning. I didn't want to go to the gym, read, or do any of the crafts I had always been so fond of. It's like I had lost the desire to do anything that would remind me of before the divorce. I was definitely in a rut.

It wasn't until my youngest daughter in college called that I had ever heard of birding. She was so excited at the program that was offered through the University that she told me all about it. After I hung up with her, I was mildly intrigued. For the first time in months, something had caught my attention to a degree. I decided I would research it later that night before bed and did just that. Soon my mild interest turned into avid curiosity. I had always loved the outdoors and wildlife, so why not take a walk and look at a few birds?

Due to a hectic work schedule, my little excursion was put off until the following weekend. I was impressed that I hadn't lost my interest in birding as I did with many other things as of late. So it was time to go for my little nature walk. I drove to the local park and began my journey. I was amazed at how many birds there were all around that I would have normally ignored. Not only were there a lot of birds, but quite a variety. I began to count the different kinds of birds that I found in trees, on the grass, in little puddles, and in bushes. After about 30 minutes of this, I realized that I was enjoying myself and really getting into it.

Finally after months of being a depressed hermit, I found a new passion. Who knew it would be birds? After an hour I drove home to call my daughter. I told her all about my little adventure in the park and all the beautiful birds I had seen. I soon found that I was excited about the subject of birds as she was. She couldn't wait until a break so that she could come home and we could go on a birding excursion together.

A few weeks passed and she came home during spring break. We had both done quite a bit of research on birding in the meantime and had all the equipment we needed. Going to a local national park, we began our quest for birds. We were both equipped with our handy notebooks and pen. The good thing is that we found tons of birds; the bad thing was that we had trouble identifying what was what. We both decided that we needed to get a little help. My daughter mentioned the birding trips that were offered at the university, and how helpful they were.

Driving home we were both contented with the amazing time we had birding, even with the identification issues. Since she had a few days left on vacation we found a local birding trip and signed up. Having people who knew what they were doing was an amazing help to both of us. Everyone was so nice and helpful; they were more than willing to share their information. It was on this trip that we met a man named Rob that kind of took us under his wing and showed us the ropes of birding. The trip was amazing and I planned to join more as they arose.

My daughter went back to school and I was left with my new hobby. I began joining organizations such as the ABA and Audubon Society. I love their magazines and newsletters. I think I have gained a bunch of my knowledge from those sources, maybe more than anywhere else. I participated in more birding trips and became good friends with many that attended them. Rob and I became betters friends and he was very helpful, always explaining things as we were birding so I could further enjoy my birding experiences.

Birding helped rescue me from a mid life crisis and the deep pit of despair that I was in. It helped to get me out of my house, among nature, and among other people who share the same interest. It was great because it was something me and my daughter can share, regardless of the vast age difference. Between my daughter and me, we've even managed to get the rest of my kids into birding to different degrees. It has brought me closer to all my children and helped me find the woman that was hiding behind my depression. Birding helped save me and has given me a great hobby to enjoy for the rest of my life.

Birding also helped me meet my new husband Rob. He's the other love in my life aside from birding. It's so great that we share the same interests. Rob and I are always going on birding trips, whether they are in a park close by, or the trip to Hawaii we took last month. The great thing about birding is that are basically birds wherever you go. It's great!

Prologue

As you the reader has read this book, you have probably have been overloaded with bird watching facts. The simple truth of bird watching is that you should be able to just go out and enjoy yourself. This is such a simple pass time that you can just sit back against a tree and watch. The recording and the logs that you keep can be as simple or as complex as you want them to be. The idea is to just enjoy the pass time and if you are one of those people who are anal about records, then the societies and the organizations listed within this text will be glad to take your data as part of records and facts.

Bird watching is more important today than ever before. As the human population grows and the delicate balance of our ecosystem is jeopardized, every eye that is watching birds is also watching for that balance to tip. If a species is being wiped out, it is the bird watchers who will have the best advantage to catch that balance for from being tipped to opposite side of the spectrum. With bird watchers in the field there are a thousand pair of eyes that are able to see the subtle changes in nuances of a species habitat and their populations.

In this aspect bird watching goes from a pastoral past time to a mandatory vigilance over the wildlife realm. As we all become guardians of our own planet the bird watchers are the first defense against total planet destruction. Other species only have biologists and other scientists to watch the population ebb and flow. The birds are lucky because thousands of people are watching birds and they watch them as they flourish are even perhaps diminish.

As an amateur birdwatcher your first duty is just to have fun, but as you get more interested in the past time you can be a valuable contributor to many elements of science. The most exciting thing for a birdwatcher to find is a species that was thought to be extinct. The joy of finding at least one bird out there where for years people thought they have died out is a feeling that can not be compared to any of other situation. Or you may be at the opposite end of that feeling when you see the last two of a species and know that their chances of survival are very poor to none at all.

Bird Watching for Beginners

Printed in Great Britain
by Amazon